ARE THEY REAL?

UFOs

by Selina Li Bi

BrightPoint Press

San Diego, CA

© 2024 BrightPoint Press
an imprint of ReferencePoint Press, Inc.
Printed in the United States

For more information, contact:
BrightPoint Press
PO Box 27779
San Diego, CA 92198
www.BrightPointPress.com

ALL RIGHTS RESERVED.

No part of this work covered by the copyright hereon may be reproduced or used in any form or by any means—graphic, electronic, or mechanical, including photocopying, recording, taping, web distribution, or information storage retrieval systems—without the written permission of the publisher.

LIBRARY OF CONGRESS CATALOGING-IN-PUBLICATION DATA

Names: Li Bi, Selina, author.
Title: UFOs / by Selina Li Bi.
Description: San Diego, CA: BrightPoint Press, [2024] | Series: Are they real? | Includes bibliographical references and index. | Audience: Ages 13 | Audience: Grades 7-9
Identifiers: LCCN 2023000082 (print) | LCCN 2023000083 (eBook) | ISBN 9781678206345 (hardcover) | ISBN 9781678206352 (eBook)
Subjects: LCSH: Unidentified flying objects--Juvenile literature.
Classification: LCC TL789.2 .B56 2024 (print) | LCC TL789.2 (eBook) | DDC 001.942--dc23/eng/20230111
LC record available at https://lccn.loc.gov/2023000082
LC eBook record available at https://lccn.loc.gov/2023000083

CONTENTS

AT A GLANCE	4
INTRODUCTION STRANGE ENCOUNTER IN THE SKIES	6
CHAPTER ONE WHAT IS A UFO?	12
CHAPTER TWO THE HISTORY OF UFOs	22
CHAPTER THREE LOOKING AT THE EVIDENCE	36
CHAPTER FOUR THE CULTURAL IMPACT OF UFOs	48
Glossary	58
Source Notes	59
For Further Research	60
Index	62
Image Credits	63
About the Author	64

AT A GLANCE

- *UFO* stands for "unidentified flying object." Sometimes these things are later identified as airplanes, drones, or other normal objects.

- Some people think UFOs are alien spacecraft. UFO sightings raise the question of life outside of Earth.

- The appearance of UFOs varies. They have been described as lights or flying objects. They have been seen in the sky and below the sea.

- People have been reporting strange things in the sky since ancient times. One of the earliest UFO sightings was in 343 BCE.

- Astronomer J. Allen Hynek grouped UFO sightings into distant and close encounters. Close encounters include people who believe they were taken onto alien UFOs.

- In 1947, pilot Kenneth Arnold saw a UFO. His descriptions of the sighting led to the term *flying saucer*.

- Another famous UFO sighting is the strange wreckage found in Roswell, New Mexico, in 1947. Some people claim it came from an alien spacecraft.

- Today, there are video recordings of UFOs. Some of these videos have been taken by US Navy pilots.

- There have been many scientific studies on UFOs. NASA formed a UFO study group in 2022.

INTRODUCTION

STRANGE ENCOUNTER IN THE SKIES

The pilot took off in an F/A-18F Super Hornet jet. His wingman flew behind him. The fighter jets could fly very fast. They were equipped with advanced **radar**.

Minutes into the flight, something caught the pilot's eye. A strange object appeared on his radar screen. The image was a bit fuzzy. It looked like an oval object in the sky.

The pilot wondered if it was a **drone**. But it didn't move like a drone. The object zipped in circles on the radar. It could move faster than anything he had seen before.

A pilot can see the radar on a screen inside the F/A-18F Super Hornet.

UFOs are sometimes spotted hovering above the sea. There have been reports of these objects diving into the water too.

"Do you see that on the radar?" the pilot asked his wingman.

"Yeah," said the wingman. "What do you think it is?"

"I have no idea," the pilot replied. "Let's go check it out." They turned and headed toward the object.

As he flew closer to the target, the pilot spotted something white hovering above the water. How did the object stay in the air? The pilot didn't see any wings or propellers.

Suddenly, the object changed directions very quickly. This was unheard of for any normal aircraft. The object whipped past the jet. Then it disappeared.

The pilot couldn't believe his eyes. Since he didn't have a name for what he saw,

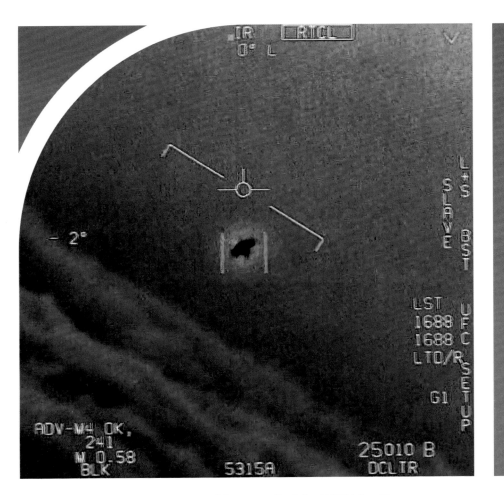

The video captured by a pilot in 2015 isn't very detailed. But it does show an unidentified object.

it would be called an unidentified flying object (UFO). Luckily, his jet was recording video the whole time. His sighting could be shared with the world.

UFO SIGHTINGS

Throughout history, people have seen objects or lights in the sky that they don't understand. UFO sightings happen all over the world. These sightings bring up many questions. Some questions are about life beyond the planet Earth.

Scientists have researched UFOs. Many organizations have been formed to investigate UFO sightings. To this day, people are curious about UFOs. They want to know what these objects are and where they come from. But do alien UFOs really exist?

1

WHAT IS A UFO?

The US Air Force created the term *UFO* in 1952. The Air Force needed to describe the strange lights or objects that people reported in the sky. Experts studied these sightings. If the experts could not explain what the mysterious object was, it was called a UFO.

APPEARANCE AND LOCATION OF UFOs

Many UFO sightings happen at night. UFOs might look like lights in the sky. These lights

Many people who report UFO sightings did not see an actual aircraft.

may move at high speeds. They might disappear and reappear. They can also change direction very quickly.

People have also seen flying objects. The reported shape of UFOs varies. The most common UFOs reported are disk shaped. The object often has a raised dome in the center. This flying saucer shape is often seen in books, movies, and video games.

UFOs are not only seen in the skies. They have been seen hovering above the sea. They may dive beneath the waves. US submarines have investigated these objects. But they haven't learned much about them.

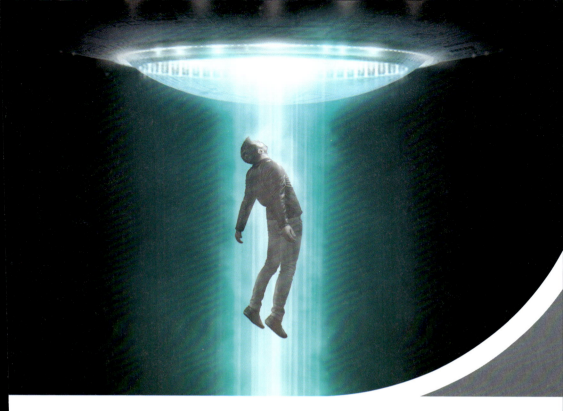

So far, there is no proof that any human has had contact with aliens.

ALIENS

UFO sightings raise the question of **extraterrestrial** life. Some people believe that UFOs are alien spacecraft. People have even reported being taken by aliens and brought onto a UFO. The experience may seem very real to the person who reported it. However, there is usually no evidence that it really happened.

CLASSIFICATION OF UFO ENCOUNTERS

Ufology is the study of UFOs. This field began in the 1900s. Ufologists are people who study these objects. They interview people who may have seen a UFO. They also review evidence such as photos or videos. Ufologists learned that some UFOs are actually planes or weather events. But other sightings are still mysteries.

Some ufologists are **conspiracy theorists**. They believe the government is hiding information about alien UFOs. These beliefs are not supported by evidence.

Other ufologists work with government agencies. An astronomer named J. Allen Hynek made a big difference in the study

SLEEP PARALYSIS

Some scientists explain that people who believe they were taken by aliens actually experienced sleep **paralysis**. This condition happens when the mind is awake but the body is still asleep. It is a dreamlike state. Sleep paralysis can be confusing and scary. People who experience it might not understand what is happening. They might think they are being abducted.

of UFOs. Starting in 1948, Hynek helped the US Air Force study UFO reports. At first, he did not believe in alien UFOs. But after studying many cases, he became very curious. Hynek became an expert on UFOs. In 1977, he said, "Today I would not spend one further moment on the subject of UFOs if I didn't seriously feel that the UFO **phenomenon** is real."[1]

Hynek collected many reports. He grouped them into distant and close encounters. Distant encounters were objects seen from far away. These could be lights in the sky or objects on radar

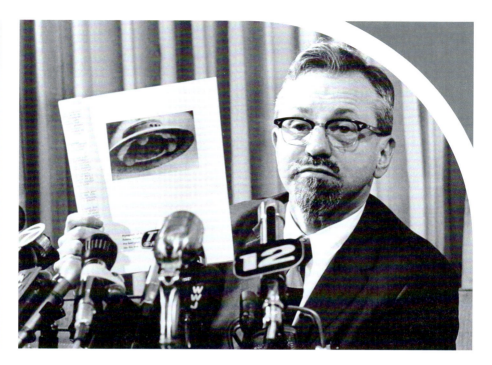

J. Allen Hynek spoke at a press conference in 1966. He dismissed UFO sightings. He would later change his opinion of these reports.

screens. Close encounters were sightings within 500 feet (150 m) of the person who saw the UFO. Hynek named three types of close encounters.

The first kind of encounters happen when a person only sees a UFO. The second kind

Crop circles are patterns cut into fields. In the past, they have mysteriously appeared on farms. Some people claim that they are evidence of UFOs.

happen when the UFO leaves evidence behind. For example, the UFO might leave a mark on the ground. The third kind happens when someone sees an alien creature.

There are many theories about UFOs. Many UFO sightings are eventually explained. Some people think all sightings have normal explanations. Yet there are plenty of reports that scientists still don't understand. Some people think that UFOs are unidentified government aircraft on secret missions. Others believe that UFOs are alien spacecraft. Many of these sightings remain a mystery.

NEW TERM FOR UFOs

Some scientists have started calling UFOs unidentified aerial phenomena (UAP). The term *UFO* has been closely linked with aliens. The new term suggests that sightings have natural causes. Some people believe the new term is necessary. It will allow scientists to take the subject more seriously.

2
THE HISTORY OF UFOs

UFO sightings have been recorded for thousands of years. They have been called many different things, from sky gods to flying saucers. Many of these sightings are still unexplained.

Early UFO sightings are often connected to myths and legends. One of the first sightings was in 343 BCE. A Greek general named Timoleon sailed the Mediterranean Sea. He was guided by a bright light.

Many strange lights that appear in the sky can be explained. Planets, stars, comets, and meteors could all be mistaken for UFOs.

He described the light as "a torch blazing in the sky."[2]

During that time, the light was seen as a guide from heaven. Some say it was probably just a comet or meteor shower. Yet there is no evidence of a comet at that time. The strange light stayed in the sky the whole night. A meteor would have been gone within minutes.

There are also ancient cave paintings that look very similar to modern-day reports of aliens seen near UFOs. In Aboriginal Australian myths, some spirits are called Wandjina. Cave paintings of Wandjina sky

The Wandjina sky spirits are often drawn with lines around their heads. This might represent a headdress, halo, or helmet.

spirits show strange beings with large eyes and no mouth. They look like alien visitors someone might think of today.

STRANGE AIRSHIPS

In the late 1890s, strange airships were seen sailing across the skies.

They were usually seen at night. Airships are aircraft such as blimps that float through the sky. Some people reported that the airships they saw also had wings. Other people claimed the airships looked like boats attached to large balloons.

In 1896, hundreds of people in California saw one of these mysterious sights in the sky. It was a slow-moving light attached to an airship. Some people heard singing coming from the airship.

There were many different explanations for the airship sightings. The first blimp was flown in 1884. Some people believed that

People drew the strange airships reported through the 1880s and 1890s. Newspapers across the United States published some of these drawings.

the strange airships were new inventions being tested. Others thought they were just false reports sent to newspapers as pranks. One man thought they were fireflies. Most of the journalists during that time did not take the reports seriously.

FOO FIGHTERS

Near the end of World War II (1939–1945), multiple air crews spotted strange sights in the night sky near the border between Germany and France. Lieutenant Fred Ringwald was part of the 415th Night Fighter Squadron. On one mission, he said, "I wonder what these lights are, over there in the hills."[3] He saw eight to ten lights in a row. They were fiery orange and glowed in the night sky. Lieutenant Ringwald was riding with another pilot. At first, the airmen thought the lights might be some sort of weapon. They turned the plane toward the

World War II pilots might have seen lights that looked like aircraft. They may have seen actual flying objects. Scientists still aren't sure how to explain their reports.

lights. They were ready to fight if they had

to. But the lights vanished.

On another night, Lieutenant

Samuel A. Krasney described seeing a

cigar-shaped object near where Lieutenant

Ringwald had seen lights. The object glowed red. It looked like it was riding just off the plane's wingtip. The object stayed with the aircraft for several minutes. Then it took off and disappeared.

Some pilots during World War II called the strange lights foo fighters. The name was inspired by an American comic strip.

ST. ELMO'S FIRE

Some people believe that pilots reporting UFOs actually saw something called St. Elmo's Fire. This is a weather phenomenon where an object glows blue during a storm. The glow comes from electricity. But the pilots said they knew what St. Elmo's Fire looked like. These lights were something different.

It was called *Smokey Stover.* It was about a fireman named Smokey. He drove a fire truck called the Foo Mobile.

Some scientists thought the foo fighters were just flares or weather balloons. The 415th aircrew did not agree. These objects seemed to track their planes. Flares and weather balloons could not do that. The objects are still unidentified.

FLYING SAUCERS

In 1947, a man named Kenneth Arnold was flying his plane near Mount Rainier in Washington. He reported seeing a group of nine objects. He thought they were moving incredibly fast. He said the lights moved "like saucers skipping on water."[4] Arnold was describing the motion of the object, not its shape. But the phrase *flying saucer* caught on as a popular description of what UFOs looked like.

UFO sightings increased. In 1947, the US Air Force began to investigate these reports. They called this investigation Project Sign. Most of the researchers thought the UFOs were some sort of high-tech aircraft. At the time, the Soviet Union was a major US rival. Some thought the sightings were

Soviet planes spying on the United States. However, a few researchers thought these flying objects were spacecraft from another world.

ROSWELL, NEW MEXICO

One of the most famous modern-day UFO reports was near Roswell, New Mexico.

PROJECT BLUE BOOK

The US Air Force's investigation into UFOs lasted from 1947 to 1969. It was later called Project Blue Book. There were 12,618 sightings reported. Researchers were able to find explanations for most of them. However, about 700 of these sightings are still unidentified.

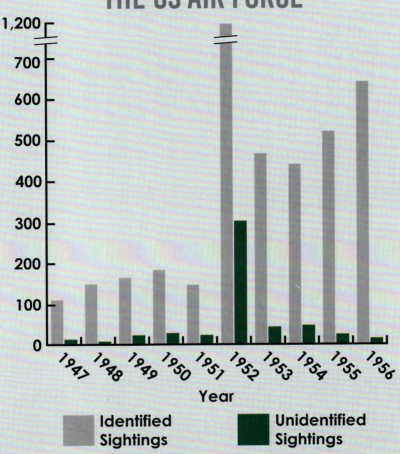

Project Sign and Project Blue Book investigated UFO sightings. The US Air Force released information about how many of those sightings were eventually explained. In the first ten years of the program, more than 500 sightings were never identified.

It happened in July 1947. A rancher named William Ware "Mac" Brazel discovered strange wreckage on his farm. **Debris** was scattered over a large area of land. That summer, there were many stories of flying saucers in the news. Brazel wondered if this wreckage might have come from a UFO.

Eventually, the US military investigated what Brazel found. But their explanations of the debris have changed many times. There are still questions about the Roswell incident today.

3
LOOKING AT THE EVIDENCE

UFOs can be hard to explain. They seem to appear out of nowhere. They rarely leave any signs. Today, videos are used to record UFO sightings. Sometimes, evidence of a UFO shows that it was really a known aircraft. However, some UFO sightings are still mysteries.

STRANGE FINDINGS AT ROSWELL

Mac Brazel told the sheriff of Roswell about the mysterious debris on his ranch. The Roswell Army Air Field became involved. Major Jesse Marcel collected samples of the debris. He was an intelligence officer. He studied the samples.

Not all evidence of UFOs is real. In 1951, the US Air Force investigated an image of a UFO. Later, the photographer revealed that the photo was faked.

Jesse Marcel visited Mac Brazel to investigate the debris. Although he took samples, none of the material has been saved today.

Marcel found tinfoil-like material. It was very thin and extremely light. It was also flexible. It looked like metal, but it acted more like plastic or rubber.

At first, the Roswell Army Air Field said that it had found a flying disc. The next day, it changed its story. It said the debris was from a weather balloon. Many years later, the US Air Force said the debris was actually from a secret spy mission called Project Mogul. The military sent balloons high into the sky to detect nuclear testing. Brazel had found wreckage from one of these balloons.

ALIEN BODIES

Some reports said that alien bodies were removed from the Roswell site. Glenn

Dennis worked at a funeral home nearby. He sometimes worked with the Roswell Army Air Field. He says that he received a few strange calls from the base. They wanted to know what chemicals to use to store a body.

In 1997, there was a follow-up report from the government. It said that the

THE UFO CITY

The city of Roswell has become famous for the UFO incident. There is a UFO Museum and Research Center. The town has a McDonald's shaped like a flying saucer. Alien-themed lights line the streets. There is even an annual UFO Festival.

The International UFO Museum and Research Center is in Roswell. The museum displays what aliens might look like.

creatures were parachute test dummies.

Some conspiracy theorists are still investigating the Roswell incident.

US NAVY PILOT VIDEOS

In 2004, Lieutenant David Fravor was leading a training mission. Fravor was flying an F/A-18F Super Hornet. His radar picked up strange objects on the horizon.

Another pilot captured a video of the plane's radar feed that night. The radar shows the object. It is a small oval with no wings. It moves quickly back and forth.

Fravor said the object copied his moves. He flew toward the object. It flew toward him. Then it disappeared. Fravor said it was "something I had never seen in my life."[5]

US Navy pilots experienced something similar a decade later. In 2014, a few Navy pilots saw unusual blurs on their radar. The shapes were round or oval. They moved in

US Navy pilots never got close enough to see details of the aircraft or object they spotted.

circular patterns. Sometimes they rotated in the air. The pilots were amazed. One pilot said, "It didn't fly like an aircraft."[6]

There were many reports of these kinds of objects. US Navy pilot Ryan Graves

Military aircraft have been mistaken for alien UFOs. Some people say the B-2 Spirit stealth bomber looks like a flying saucer in the air.

said that these UFOs "were pretty much always there when we went out."[7] There were times when the jets almost ran into the objects. The pilots and their commanders were concerned about safety and national security. But they never found out what the objects were.

POSSIBLE EXPLANATIONS

The Navy pilots who saw these objects had a few ideas about what they could be. Some believed the UFOs were secret US aircraft. Others thought they were foreign spy technology. The pilots might have seen secret aircraft missions. But some people still think there is an alien explanation.

Luis Elizondo was a military intelligence official. Part of his job was to study UFOs. He explained that several things set UFOs apart from known aircraft. UFOs can fly without wings. They can quickly change directions. UFOs move without leaving behind a vapor trail or making sonic booms. It's hard to get a clear view of them, even with high-tech equipment.

REAL-WORLD UFO BELIEVERS

There are many people who believe in alien UFOs. The Mutual UFO Network (MUFON) was founded in 1969. It is one of the oldest and largest UFO groups in the world. It has

SCIENTIFIC PURSUITS OF UFOs

There have been serious scientific searches for UFOs. The hunt for UFOs continued into the 2020s. In July 2022, NASA officially formed a study team. The team planned to examine UFO sightings. It wanted to use data and evidence to understand what UFOs really are.

a Science Review Board. Scientists collect data about UFO sightings and study them.

Dr. Steven Greer is an American ufologist. He founded the Center for the Study of Extraterrestrial Intelligence (CSETI). CSETI believes that aliens visit Earth. It believes in a peaceful relationship with them. There are many individuals who study UFOs as well.

In 2022, military reports of UFO sightings grew. There were around 400 reports. The US Congress held a meeting with top military officials to discuss sightings. Government research into UFOs is likely to continue.

4
THE CULTURAL IMPACT OF UFOs

The idea of UFOs remains popular. There are many science fiction books about UFOs and aliens. They are a part of movies, television shows, and video games.

RADIO BROADCAST PANIC

On October 30, 1938, actor Orson Welles broadcast a radio show. It was based on a science fiction novel called *The War of the Worlds* by H.G. Wells. The book was about Martians invading Earth. Welles warned listeners that it was fiction. But not everyone heard that warning.

The War of the Worlds *was reprinted many times. In 1927, it was published in* Amazing Stories. *The magazine's cover illustrated an alien attack.*

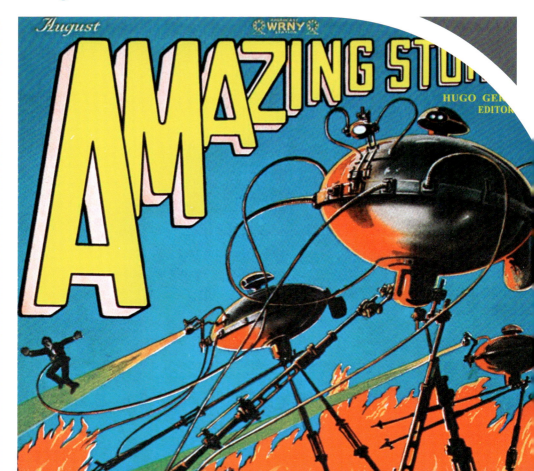

The radio show started with regular music. But the songs were sometimes interrupted by a reporter. Each time, the reporter talked about an ongoing alien attack. Thousands of listeners believed there truly was an invasion. This led to panic. Welles hadn't meant to cause a panic. But the performance showed that lots of people could believe in aliens.

FILM

UFOs have been the subject of many famous movies. Aliens are often shown as something to fear. They are creatures

E.T. has the characteristics of many pop-culture aliens. He has a large head and big eyes. But he looks more friendly than others.

who want to take over the world. However, in one movie, director Steven Spielberg showed aliens in a different way.

Spielberg made a movie called *E.T. the Extra-Terrestrial* (1982). In the movie,

E.T. is a gentle alien. He makes friends with humans instead of hurting them. The movie was a huge hit. It made millions of dollars and won four Academy Awards.

Independence Day is a 1996 science fiction action film. Giant flying saucers appear above cities. The aliens threaten to take over Earth. Humans must find a way to

ALIEN BEINGS

Aliens across pop culture look very different. Some aliens are short and green, with giant heads and eyes. Others have gray skin and long arms and legs. But most aliens look a little bit like humans. This helps people recognize and understand aliens. It makes them more believable.

fight back. *The Tomorrow War* is a science fiction action film from 2021. Time travelers visit Earth to say there will be a war against aliens. People travel to the future to battle the aliens. These movies show a more violent approach to contact with aliens.

TELEVISION

Many television series show UFOs. One famous example is *The X-Files*. The show is a science fiction drama about two FBI special agents. They investigate unsolved **paranormal** cases. One agent believes in the paranormal. The other is a medical

Space Invaders *was inspired in part by the book* The War of the Worlds, *the same story featured on Orson Welles's radio show.*

doctor. She needs more evidence to believe such things. Together, they solve cases called X-Files.

The television series became a hit. The show aired from 1993 to 2002. There were additional episodes in 2016 and 2018. The series won five Golden Globe Awards.

VIDEO GAMES

Video games can take players to different worlds. For years, aliens have been a popular topic. Many of the games have cool weapons and gadgets to fight the aliens.

An early alien-themed video game was *Space Invaders*. It was released in 1978. It is a simple game. A player must shoot rows of aliens on the screen and avoid being shot. It inspired many video games to come.

The *Halo* series is a popular science fiction action series that started in 2001. It is about humans fighting against different alien species. *Destroy All Humans* is a video game series first released in 2005. The player controls a large-headed alien.

UFOs are commonly seen in popular media. Movies and TV shows give possible answers to real-world questions about UFOs. In video games, players can feel what an alien invasion might be like. But for now, aliens only exist in these kinds of media. There is no clear evidence of real alien UFOs.

Reports of UFO sightings continue throughout the world. Some mysterious flying objects remain unidentified. Some people believe alien UFOs are not real.

Popular media will continue to explore UFOs and the possibilities of alien life-forms.

Yet the possibility of extraterrestrial life still exists. Scientists and UFO organizations are still searching for answers.

GLOSSARY

conspiracy theorists

people who believe in secret plans

debris

material left behind in a crash

drone

an aircraft that does not have a pilot on board

extraterrestrial

something that is not from Earth

paralysis

a state in which a person or thing cannot move

paranormal

something that is unexplained by science, such as ghosts or aliens

phenomenon

an extraordinary or surprising event

radar

a system that sends out signals and detects the reflection of those signals after they bounce off objects

SOURCE NOTES

CHAPTER ONE: WHAT IS A UFO?

1. J. Allen Hynek, *The Hynek UFO Report: The Authoritative Account of the Project Blue Book Cover-Up*. Newburyport, MA: Red Wheel/Weiser, 2020. p. 20.

CHAPTER TWO: THE HISTORY OF UFOs

2. Quoted in Jacques Valee and Chris Aubeck, *Wonders in the Sky: Unexplained Aerial Objects from Antiquity to Modern Times*. New York: Penguin, 2010. p. 46.

3. Quoted in Adam Janos, "Mysterious UFOs Seen by WWII Airman Still Unexplained," *History*, January 15, 2020. www.history.com.

4. Quoted in "History of UFOs," *History*, September 11, 2019. www.history.com.

CHAPTER THREE: LOOKING AT THE EVIDENCE

5. Quoted in Adam Janos, "Former Navy Pilot: UFO 'Something I Had Never Seen in My Life,'" *CNN*, December 20, 2017. www.cnn.com.

6. Quoted in Greg Daugherty and Missy Sullivan, "These 5 UFO Traits, Captured on Video by Navy Fighters, Defy Explanation," *History*, June 5, 2019. www.history.com.

7. Quoted in Marik Von Rennenkampff, "Stunned by UFOs, 'Exasperated' Fighter Pilots Get Little Help from Pentagon," *The Hill*, July 7, 2022. www.thehill.com.

FOR FURTHER RESEARCH

BOOKS

Craig Boutland, *Scary Alien Abductions*. Minneapolis, MN: Lerner Publications, 2019.

Tom Jackson, *Are We Alone in the Universe? Theories About Intelligent Life on Other Planets.* New York: Gareth Stevens Publishing, 2019.

Yvette LaPierre, *The Bermuda Triangle*. San Diego, CA: BrightPoint Press, 2024.

INTERNET SOURCES

"Outer Space 101: What Exactly Are UFOs?" *CBC Kids*, June 26, 2021. www.cbc.ca.

"Unidentified Flying Object (UFO)," *Britannica Kids*, 2022. https://kids.britannica.com.

"U.S. Military Releases UFO Videos to Prove They're Real," *Kids News*, April 29, 2020. www.kidsnews.com.

WEBSITES

Boeing F/A-18 Super Hornet
www.boeing.com/defense/fa-18-super-hornet/

Boeing's website about the F/A-18 Super Hornet includes information about the aircraft and stories from its pilots.

European Space Agency
www.esa.int/kids/en/news

The European Space Agency has a fun website with space news, animations, downloads, and contests.

NASA Solar System Exploration
https://solarsystem.nasa.gov/solar-system/our-solar-system/overview/

NASA's Solar System Exploration page is a place to check out real objects in the night sky.

INDEX

abduction, 15–16, 17
airships, 25–27
aliens, 11, 15–18, 20–21, 24–25, 39–41, 45, 46–47, 48–53, 55–57
Arnold, Kenneth, 31–32

Brazel, William Ware "Mac," 35, 37, 39

Center for the Study of Extraterrestrial Intelligence (CSETI), 47
close encounters, 18–19
conspiracy theorists, 17, 41

Dennis, Glen, 39–40
distant encounters, 18–19

Elizondo, Luis, 45–46
E.T. the Extra-Terrestrial, 51–52

flying saucer, 14, 22, 32, 35, 40, 52
foo fighters, 30–31
Fravor, David, 41–42

Graves, Ryan, 43–44

Hynek, J. Allen, 17–19

Krasney, Samuel A., 29–30

Marcel, Jesse, 37–38
meteors, 24
Mutual UFO Network (MUFON), 46

Project Blue Book, 33, 34
Project Mogul, 39
Project Sign, 32, 34

radar, 6–8, 18–19, 42
Ringwald, Fred, 28, 29–30
Roswell Army Air Field, 37–39, 40
Roswell incident, 33–35, 37–41

sleep paralysis, 17
Soviet Union, 32–33
St. Elmo's Fire, 30

Timoleon, 23–24

ufologists, 16–18, 47
unidentified arial phenomena (UAP), 21
US Air Force, 12, 18, 32, 33, 34, 39
US Navy, 42–45

Wandjina cave paintings, 24–25
weather balloons, 31, 39
weather phenomena, 16, 30
Welles, Orson, 48–50
Wells, H.G., 49
World War II, 28, 30

X-Files, The, 53–54

IMAGE CREDITS

Cover: © Marko Aliaksandr/Shutterstock Images
5: © ktsdesign/Shutterstock Images
7: © Mass Communication Specialist 2nd Class Ron Kuzlik/US Navy
8: © Ursatii/Shutterstock Images
10: © Department of Defense/AP Images
13: © WeAre/Shutterstock Images
15: © MyImages-Micha/Shutterstock Images
19: © Alvin Quinn/AP Images
20: © YueStock/Shutterstock Images
23: © iiievgeniy/iStockphoto
25: © ChameleonsEye/Shutterstock Images
27: © *The Saint Paul Globe*
29: © IgorZh/Shutterstock Images
34: © Red Line Editorial
37: © US Air Force/National Archives Museum
38: © Universal History Archive/Universal Images Group/Getty Images
41: © CrackerClips Stock Media/Shutterstock Images
43: © simonbradfield/iStockphoto
44: © Senior Airman Eugene Oliver/501st Combat Support Wing Public Affairs/US Air Force/DVIDS
49: © Frank R. Paul/*Amazing Stories*
51: © Ewa Studio/Shutterstock Images
54: © ilbusca/iStockphoto
57: © Rastan/iStockphoto

ABOUT THE AUTHOR

Selina Li Bi enjoys writing about things that make her curious. She practiced as an eye doctor for many years. She holds degrees in biology and creative writing. She writes nonfiction and fiction with two loyal pups by her side.